First Print Edition [1.0] -1437h. (2016 c.e.)

Copyright © 1437 H./2016 C.E.
Taalib al-Ilm Educational Resources

http://taalib.com
Learn Islaam, Live Islaam.^{SM}

ISBN EAN-13:   978-1-938117-70-1 [Soft cover Print Edition]

GOLDEN WORDS UPON GOLDEN WORDS...FOR EVERY MUSLIM.

"Imaam al-Barbahaaree, may Allaah have mercy upon him said:

May Allaah have mercy upon you! Examine carefully the speech of everyone you hear from in your time particularly. So do not act in haste and do not enter into anything from it until you ask and see: Did any of the Companions of the Prophet, may Allaah's praise and salutations be upon him, speak about it, or did any of the scholars? So if you find a narration from them about it, cling to it, do not go beyond it for anything and do not give precedence to anything over it and thus fall into the Fire.

Explanation by Sheikh Saaleh al-Fauzaan, may Allaah preserve him:

'Do not be hasty in accepting as correct what you may hear from the people especially in these later times. As now there are many who speak about so many various matters, issuing rulings and ascribing to themselves both knowledge and the right to speak. This is especially the case after the emergence and spread of new modern day media technologies. Such that everyone now can speak and bring forth that which is in truth worthless; by this meaning words of no true value - speaking about whatever they wish in the name of knowledge and in the name of the religion of Islaam. It has even reached the point that you find the people of misguidance and the members of the various groups of misguidance and deviance from the religion speaking as well. Such individuals have now become those who speak in the name of the religion of Islaam through means such as the various satellite television channels. Therefore be very cautious!

It is upon you oh Muslim, and upon you oh student of knowledge individually, to verify matters and not rush to embrace everything and anything you may hear. It is upon you to verify the truth of what you hear, asking, 'Who else also makes this same statement or claim?', 'Where did this thought or concept originate or come from?', 'Who is its reference or source authority?'. Asking what are the evidences which support it from within the Book and the Sunnah? And inquiring where has the individual who is putting this forth studied and taken his knowledge from? From who has he studied the knowledge of Islaam?

Each of these matters requires verification through inquiry and investigation, especially in the present age and time. As it is not every speaker who should rightly be considered a source of knowledge, even if he is well spoken and eloquent, and can manipulate words captivating his listeners. Do not be taken in and accept him until you are aware of the degree and scope of what he possesses of knowledge and understanding. As perhaps someone's words may be few, but possess true understanding, and perhaps another will have a great deal of speech yet he is actually ignorant to such a degree that he doesn't actually posses anything of true understanding. Rather he only has the ability to enchant with his speech so that the people are deceived. Yet he puts forth the perception that he is a scholar, that he is someone of true understanding and comprehension, that he is a capable thinker, and so forth. Through such means and ways he is able to deceive and beguile the people, taking them away from the way of truth.

Therefore what is to be given true consideration is not the amount of the speech put forth or that one can extensively discuss a subject. Rather the criterion that is to be given consideration is what that speech contains within it of sound authentic knowledge, what it contains of the established and transmitted principles of Islaam. As perhaps a short or brief statement which is connected to or has a foundation in the established principles can be of greater benefit than a great deal of speech which simply rambles on, and through hearing you don't actually receive very much benefit from.

This is the reality which is present in our time; one sees a tremendous amount of speech which only possesses within it a small amount of actual knowledge. We see the presence of many speakers yet few people of true understanding and comprehension.' "

[The eminent major scholar Sheikh Saaleh al-Fauzaan, may Allaah preserve him- 'A Valued Gift for the Reader Of Comments Upon the Book Sharh as-Sunnah', page 102-103]

This pocket edition is a selection taken from the larger book:

Statements of the Guiding Scholars of Our Age Regarding Books & their Advice to the Beginner Seeker of Knowledge

With Selections from the Following Scholars:

Sheikh 'Abdul-'Azeez ibn 'Abdullah ibn Baaz -Sheikh Muhammad ibn Saaleh al-'Utheimein - Sheikh Muhammad Naasiruddeen al-Albaanee - Sheikh Muqbil ibn Haadee al-Waada'ee - Sheikh 'Abdur-Rahman ibn Naaser as-Sa'adee - Sheikh Muhammad 'Amaan al-Jaamee - Sheikh Muhammad al-Ameen as-Shanqeetee - Sheikh Ahmad ibn Yahya an-Najmee

(May Allaah have mercy upon them.) &

Sheikh Saaleh al-Fauzaan ibn 'Abdullah al-Fauzaan - Sheikh Saaleh ibn 'Abdul-'Azeez Aal-Sheikh - Sheikh Muhammad ibn 'Abdul-Wahhab al-Wasaabee -Permanent Committee to Scholastic Research & Issuing Of Islamic Rulings

(May Allaah preserve them.)

With an introduction by:
Sheikh Muhammad Ibn 'Abdullah al-Imaam
Collected and Translated
by Abu Sukhailah Khalil Ibn-Abelahyi al-Amreekee

[Available: **Now**¦ pages: **370+**
price: (Soft cover) **$25**
(Hard cover) **$32**
(eBook) **$9.99**]

A TREASURY OF GUIDANCE FOR THE MUSLIM STRIVING TO LEARN HIS RELIGION:
SHEIKH SAALEH IBN 'ABDUL-'AZEEZ AAL-SHEIKH

Statements of the Guiding Scholars Pocket Edition 6

Translated & Compiled By
Abu Sukhailah Khalil Ibn-Abelahyi al-Amreekee

Table of Contents

Images of handwritten original introduction of Sheikh Muhammad Ibn 'Abdullah al-Imaam (may Allaah preserve him)

بسم الله الرحمن الرحيم

دار الحديث للعلوم الشرعية
محمد بن عبدالله الإمام

التاريخ ١٨ / ٧ / ١٤٢٥هـ

الحمد لله والصلاة والسلام على رسول الله وعلى آله وصحبه

أما بعد

لقد اطلعت على الأخ / خليل بن إبراهيم حفظه الله على ما به من أنه جمع كلام بعض اهل العلم في الكتب التي ينصح المسلمون بقراءتها والكتب التي حذر المسلمون من قراءتها فرأيته قد جمع جمعاً طيباً ضيراً اهل العلم فما اسأل المسؤول أن ينفع بذلك وهذا من فضل الله على أن جعل الفاضل المذكور رأى أعلى أن يكون والأعمال الخير متفقاً مع الرسول صلى الله عليه وسلم «من سن في الإسلام سنة حسنة فله أجرها وأجر من عمل بها»

اليمن - لواء ذمار - معبر - هاتف : ٤٣٠٥٢١ - تليفاكس : ٤٣٠٢٨٠ - ص . ب : ٨٦٠٠١

Images of handwritten original introduction of Sheikh Muhammad Ibn 'Abdullah al-Imaam (may Allaah preserve him)

INTRODUCTION OF
SHEIKH MUHAMMAD IBN 'ABDULLAH AL-IMAAM
(MAY ALLAAH PRESERVE HIM)

All praise is due to Allaah, may Allaah's praise and His salutations be upon the Messenger of Allaah, his family, and Companions.

As for what follows:

The brother Khalil Ibn-Abelahyi, may Allaah preserve him, has shown to me that which he has undertaken in gathering the speech of some of the people of knowledge regarding the books the Muslims are advised to read, as well as those books that the Muslims are warned against reading.

After reading it, I see that he has compiled a collection from the statements of well-known people of knowledge, and he has selected well and brought forth good for the Muslims in what he presents to them in this blessed book. How can this not be so, when the foundation of every good is in reading the book that possesses benefit and in having a righteous teacher? As the scholars have mentioned, "*The one who carefully selects his teacher and his book has protected his religion with the best of safeguards.*"

Sheikh Ibn-'Utheimeen, may Allaah have mercy upon him, was asked, "At whose hands should we take knowledge?" He replied, "*From the one of correct beliefs, sound methodology, and the proper goal and objective.*" Likewise, the author of the 'Risaa'il al-Islaah' stated,

"*The rectification of the Muslim nation is through the correction of its deeds and endeavors, and the correction of its deeds and endeavors is based upon the rectification of its branches of knowledge, and the rectification of its branches of knowledge lies in the reliable transmitters of its knowledge.*" Consider what Ibn Taymeeyah has said regarding Abee Haamed al-Ghazaalee: "*The book ash-Shifaa' caused him to become afflicted...*" (Majmu'a al-Fatawaa, Vol. 10, Page 552). Meaning that the illness of Abu Haamed originated from the reading and studying the book ash-Shifaa' of Ibn Sinaa, due to what it contains of deviations that lead one outside of Islaam. May Allaah be generous to the one who said:

We ceased our brotherhood with those
　　　　who became diseased from the Book Ash-Shifaa'
And how many times have I said, oh people you are
　　　　on the very edge of the cliff because of the book
　　　　Ash- Shifaa' '
When they dismissed our warning to them
　　　　we return in death, back to Allaah with Him being
　　　　sufficient for us,
Yet they then died upon the religion of Ibn Rustaalas!
　　　　while we lived upon the way of the chosen Messenger.

(*Majmu'a al-Fatawaa, Vol. 9, Page 253*)

Therefore from the completeness of a Muslim's protection from harm and trials is that he does not acquire a book or choose it for reading or study until he inquires about that book from someone whom he knows is reliable in both his religion and his knowledge.

How many diseases of our Muslim nation are caused by reading books that are not truly reliable when judging according to the guidance of the Sharee'ah! Therefore as a statement of ample warning regarding every book in which its harm is known to be greater than its good, it is not permissible to publish it, read it, or give it as a gift.

As for the books of the sects of the Raafidhah, the Sufeeyah, the people of philosophical argument and false rhetoric- then it should be known assuredly that their evil and harm is significantly greater than any good within them. So from the completeness of a Muslim's protecting himself from harm and trials is that he does not acquire a book or choose it for reading or study until he inquires about that book from someone whom he knows is reliable regarding his religion and knowledge.

Written by
Muhammad Ibn 'Abdullah al-Imaam

COMPILER'S INTRODUCTION
(POCKET EDITION)

In the name of Allaah, The Most Gracious, The Most Merciful

Verily, all praise is due to Allaah, we praise Him, we seek His assistance and we ask for His forgiveness. We seek refuge in Him from the evils of our souls and the evils of our actions. Whoever Allaah guides, no one can lead him astray and whoever is caused to go astray, there is no one that can guide him. I bear witness that there is no deity worthy of worship except Allaah alone with no partners. And I bear witness that Muhammad is His worshipper and Messenger.

Oh you who believe, fear Allaah as He ought to be feared and do not die except while you are Muslims. -(Surah Aal-'Imraan:102)

Oh mankind, fear Allaah who created you from a single soul and from that, He created its mate. And from them He brought forth many men and women. And fear Allaah to whom you demand your mutual rights. Verily, Allaah is an ever All-Watcher over you. -(Surah an-Nisaa:1)

Oh you who believe, fear Allaah and speak a word that is truthful (and to the point) - He will rectify your deeds and forgive you your sins. And whoever obeys Allaah and His Messenger has achieved a great success. -(Surah al-Ahzaab:70-71)

As for what follows:

The best speech is the book of Allaah, and the best guidance is the guidance of Muhammad, may Allaah's praise and His salutations be upon him. And the worst of affairs are newly invented matters in the religion, and every newly invented matter in an innovation, and every innovation is a going astray, and every going astray is in the Fire.

Certainly, every Muslim hopes for success and happiness in this world and the Hereafter. Our Lord has taught us to ask Him for guidance in the "Mother" of al-Qur'aan, Surah al-Faatihah, where He explains to us exactly which path is the true path to contentment and the true way of success. The guiding scholar Sheikh 'Abdul-'Azeez Ibn 'Abdullah Ibn Baaz, may Allaah have mercy upon him, comprehensively described this path to happiness:

> "…the path to happiness and the path to success is the path which was taken by the first believers, the Companions of the Prophet, may Allaah's praise and His salutations be upon him, and those who followed them in goodness. As Allaah, the Majestic and the Exalted, says, ❦ ... **this is my straight path. Follow it and do not follow the other paths as they will separate you from His path. This is what he has ordained for you, in order that you may become righteous.**❧–(Surah al-Anaam: 153) The path of Allaah is knowledge, this truly is His path, this truly is guidance, this truly is Islaam, this truly is goodness, and this truly is the fear of Allaah.
>
> Regarding this, Allaah, Glorified and Exalted, says in Surah al-Faatihah, ❦**Guide us to the straight path.**❧ Our Lord has instructed us to ask for this; instructed that we ask from Him guidance to His straight path. And His straight path is that knowledge that was brought by His Messenger, as well as acting according to that."[1]

The hadeeth scholar Sheikh Hamaad Ibn al-Ansaaree, may Allaah have mercy upon him, explained the meaning this verse, ❦ **Guide us to the straight path** ❧ which is recited by all of us in our ritual prayers:

---

[1] From our sheikh's comments upon "Understanding of the Religion' by Sheikh Saaleh al-Fauzaan

*"The meaning of ❧ **Guide us to the straight path** ❧ is: Our Lord whom we have praised by means of what You have taught us. We ask You and supplicate to You by this supplication, which You have taught us, that You guide us to the straight path. And the meaning of ❧ **Guide us to the straight path** ❧ is: Teach us that which will benefit us, and then grant us success to act in accordance with that which benefits us."* [2]

Indeed, from the greatest means to achieving this foundation of success and happiness; is the seeking of beneficial knowledge and acting according to it. As was mentioned by Sheikh al-Islaam Ibn Taymeeyah, may Allaah have mercy upon him:

*"The seeking of Sharee'ah knowledge is generally a communal obligation upon the Muslims together collectively, except for that which has been specified as an obligation for each and every individual. For example, the seeking of knowledge of what Allaah has commanded everyone in general and what He has forbidden for them. The obtainment of that type of knowledge is considered an obligation upon every individual. As it has been narrated in the two 'Saheeh' collections from the Prophet, may Allaah's praise and His salutations be upon him, that he said, {**The one whom Allaah intends good for He gives him understanding of his religion.**}"* [3] [4]

---

[2]   Risaa'il feel-Aqeedah: page 22

[3]   This hadeeth {*The one whom Allaah intends...*} is found in Saheeh al-Bukhaaree: 71, 3116, 7312/ Saheeh Muslim: 1037/ Sunan Ibn Maajah: 221/ al-Muwatta Maalik: 1300, 1667/ Musnad Imaam Ahmad: 16395, 16404, and other narrations/ Musannaf Ibn Abee Shaaybah: 31792/ & Sunan ad-Daramee: 224, 226/- on the authority of Mu'aweeyah. And it is found in Jaame' al-Tirmidhee: 2645/ Musnad Imaam Ahmad: 2786/ & Sunan ad-Daaramee: 270, 2706/- on the authority of Ibn Abbaas. And it is found in Sunan Ibn Maajah: 220/ & Musannaf 'Abdul-Razzaaq: 30851/- on the authority of Abee Hurairah. It was declared authentic by Sheikh al-Albanee in Saheeh al-Aadab al-Mufrad: 517, Silsilat al-Hadeeth as-Saheehah: 1194, 1195, 1196, Saheeh at-Targheeb at-Tarheeb: 67, as well as in other of his books. Sheikh Muqbil declared it authentic in al-Jaame' al-Saheeh: 9, 3123, 4650, may Allaah have mercy upon them both

[4]   Majmu'a al-Fatawaa: vol. 28/80

The guiding scholar Sheikh Ibn Baaz, may Allaah have mercy upon him, explained the meaning of "Sharee'ah" knowledge:

"Knowledge is known to possess many merits. Certainly the noblest field of knowledge which the seekers can strive towards, and those who aspire can endeavor to reach, is gaining Sharee'ah knowledge. While the term 'knowledge' is used generally to refer to many things, within the statements of the scholars of Islaam what is intended by 'knowledge' is Sharee'ah knowledge. This is the meaning of knowledge in its general usage as expressed in the Book of Allaah and in the texts of the Sunnah of His Messenger, may Allaah's praise and His salutations be upon him. This is knowledge of Allaah and His names and attributes, knowledge of His right over those He created, and of what commands He legislated for them, Glorified and Exalted is He. It is knowledge of the true way and path, that which leads and directs toward Him, as well as its specific details. It is knowledge of the final state and destination in the next life of all those beings He created. This is Sharee'ah knowledge, and it is the highest type of knowledge. It is worthy of being sought after and its achievement should be aspired to.

Through this knowledge one understands who Allaah, Glorified and Exalted, is, and by means of it you are able to worship Him. Through this knowledge you understand what Allaah has permitted and what He has prohibited, what He is pleased with and what He is displeased with. And through this knowledge you understand the destiny of this life and its inevitable conclusion. That being that a group of the people will end in Paradise, achieving happiness, and the rest of the people, who are indeed the majority, will end in Hellfire, the abode of disgrace and misery." [5]

---

[5]   From a lecture given by the eminent scholar at the Islamic University in Medinah on 3/26/1404

Therefore, it becomes clear that this desired goal which leads to true success, as has been mentioned, is only possible through the seeking of beneficial knowledge, meaning Sharee'ah knowledge, from its carriers- the scholars. Similarly, what is meant by the term 'scholars' are those people of knowledge from the saved and victorious group of Muslims who have always remained upon the guidance of the Messenger, may Allaah's praise and His salutations be upon him and his Companions, inwardly and outwardly, in every generation and age. They are the people of true guidance, the well-grounded scholars of Ahlus-Sunnah wa al-Jama'ah from the early generations, the later generations, and our present day scholars.

We must recognize them and affirm their position, defend their honor, and strive to assist and cooperate with them because they carry and preserve the inheritance of the Messenger of Allaah, may Allaah's praise and salutations be upon him. Sheikh al-Islaam Ibn Taymeeyah mentioned in his book, '*Lifting the Blame*', Page 10:

"It is obligatory upon the Muslims after loyalty to Allaah the Exalted and His Messenger, to have loyalty to the believers, as is mentioned in the Qur'aan. This is especially true in regard to the scholars, as they are the inheritors of the prophets and are those who have been placed in a position by Allaah like the stars by which we are guided through the darkness of land and sea.

The Muslims are in consensus regarding their guidance and knowledge. Since in every nation before the sending of our Prophet Muhammad, may Allaah's praise and His salutations be upon him, their scholars were indeed the worst of their people, until the time of the Muslim Ummah; as certainly the scholars of the Muslims are the best of them. They are the successors of the Messenger, may Allaah's praise and His salutations be upon him, in his nation, and they give life to that which has died from his Sunnah..."

It is necessary that every Muslim understand the importance of the role of the scholars and their position in our lives, being connected to them, and listening to their advice and guidance. Thereafter, it is upon us to maintain as strong connection and relationship to them as possible. Additionally, it is necessary for us to be aware of the deception, delusions, and falsehoods of those who strive to separate or distance the Muslims from our scholars, specifically coming from those people of division and group partisanship who falsely accuse the scholars of not understanding the current situation of the world, among their other false claims. They are the ones who fail to give the scholars their proper position among the people nor acknowledge their rights upon the people. The guiding scholar Saaleh al-Fauzaan, may Allaah preserve him, stated in his book, '*The Obligation of Confirming Affairs and Honoring the Scholars and an Explanation of their Position in this Ummah*' (Page 45):

> "*Specifically, we hear this in our time and age from those who speak attacking their honor and who falsely accuse the scholars of ignorance, short-sightedness and a lack of understanding of current affairs, as they claim; and this is a very dangerous matter. Because if we are deprived of the reliable ones from the Muslim scholars, who will lead the Muslim Ummah? Who will be turned to for rulings and judgments?*

> *And I believe this to be a devised plan from our enemies. This is a plan which has deceived many who do not properly understand matters and those who do possess an intense love and strong enthusiasm for Islaam, but which is only based upon ignorance. So they have intense love and strong enthusiasm for Islaam, but the matter is not that simple. Since the most highly honored position in this Ummah is that of the scholars. It is not permitted to disparage them or accuse them of ignorance and short-sightedness, or with*

seeking the pleasure of the rulers or to describe them as the 'scholars of the rulers' or other such descriptions. This is extremely dangerous, oh worshiper of Allaah! So let us fear Allaah in regard to this matter and take caution. Clearly, it is as the poet said,

Oh scholars of the religion, oh 'salt' of the land,

What will rectify our affair, if the 'salt' itself is corrupt?'
Therefore this connection and relationship between the Muslim and the scholar is a necessity for every Muslim and especially for the beginning student of knowledge. The esteemed major scholar Sheikh Muqbil Ibn Haadee al-Waadiee, may Allaah have mercy on him, stated in '*Tuhfat al-Mujeeb 'alaa Asilaat al-Hadhar wa Ghareeb*' (Page 181-182):

"...So the cure is in returning to the Book of Allaah and the Sunnah of the Messenger of Allaah, may Allaah's praise and His salutations be upon him and his household, and then by returning to the scholars. As Allaah says, ❖ ***And when there came to them a matter concerning (public) security or fear, they announced it to the people. But if only they had referred it back to the Messenger or to those charged with authority amongst them, those who have the ability to derive a proper conclusion from it would have understood it.*** ❖*-(Surah an-Nisaa:83)   Therefore it is an obligation upon us to turn to the scholars in our affairs:* ❖***These are the parables that We send forth to the people, yet no one (truly) understands them except those with knowledge.'*** ❖*-(Surah al-'Ankaboot: 43)*

But what you see is some of the people merely memorizing three or four subjects and then taking that to the masjids, thrusting themselves forward and confronting others. Then his companions designate him 'Sheikh al-Islaam'! Is this to be considered knowledge?!?

Rather, the matter of knowledge is sitting upon a mat with your legs beneath you, being patient with the necessary hunger and poverty that comes with seeking knowledge. Consider the state of the Companions of the Messenger of Allaah, may Allaah's praise and His salutations be upon him and his household, and what they were patient in the face of.

*In addition, the people of knowledge- they are the ones who put matters in their proper places, as established in the previous noble verse where Allaah, the One free from imperfection and Exalted says,❀ **Verily, in that is a reminder to those who possess knowledge.** ❀-(Surah ar-Room: 22)'"*

In summarizing what has been mentioned of the importance of this relationship between the worshippers of Allaah and the guiding scholars, the major scholar Sheikh al-Fauzaan, may Allaah preserve him, said in his book, *'Explanation of the Mistakes of Some Authors'* (Page 18):

"Oh Muslim youth! Oh students of knowledge! Connect yourselves to your scholars, attach yourselves to them, and take knowledge from them. Attach yourselves to the reliable scholars well known for the correctness of their beliefs and the soundness of their methodology, in order that you may take knowledge from them and establish your connection with your Prophet, may Allaah's praise and His salutations be upon him, as your pious predecessors did. The Muslims have never ceased receiving this knowledge from their Prophet, through their scholars, generation after every generation."

And if one were to ask: "Who are the reliable well-known scholars?' meaning by this those well grounded in knowledge? Imaam Ibn-Qayyim, may Allaah have mercy upon him, stated:

"The one who is well grounded in knowledge; if he is confronted with uncertain matters as numerous as the waves of the ocean, his certainty and steadfastness is not affected nor diminished, nor is he afflicted by doubt. As he is steadfast and well grounded in his knowledge, he is not disturbed by such uncertainties and doubts. Rather, what occurs with one such as this is in fact the repulsion of doubts due to his being safeguarded by his knowledge and the disturbances are thus bound and subdued...." [6]

Certainly, Allaah facilitated for me the compilation of some of the statements of advice from the scholars regarding seeking knowledge and beneficial books, as well as their warnings against books containing misguidance. Initially, this was simply to remove ignorance from myself and the members of my family, and then afterwards also for my brothers and sisters who are also seeking knowledge. This is in order that we all are able to strive to proceed with correct methods and manners in our seeking of beneficial knowledge. This was accomplished only with the assistance of Allaah, the Most Generous.

I ask Allaah the Majestic to make this effort purely for His sake, and to accept it from me. I hope that this will be a beneficial book in this subject and area, for the one who seeks adherence to the religion of truth through the learning of beneficial knowledge -wherever they may be in the world. As was mentioned by Sheikh al-Islaam Ibn Taymeeyah, may Allaah the Exalted have mercy upon him, understanding the nature and source of beneficial knowledge is essential to obtaining it:

"...As for which books can be utilized and relied upon in the various areas of knowledge, then this is an extensive matter. Additionally, this differs according to the differences among the young people within a certain land. Since what has been made easy for them in some lands, from

[6]   Miftah Dar as-Sa'dah: vol. 1 page 442

knowledge, its path, and its study; has not been made possible for others in different lands. But, gather whatever goodness is possible by turning to Allaah, the Most Perfect, for assistance in acquiring the transmitted knowledge from the Prophet, may Allaah's praise and salutations be upon him. As this is what is truly entitled to be called knowledge.

As for other matters besides that, either it is knowledge but it is not truly beneficial, or that which is not actually knowledge but only mistakenly considered to be. Indeed if it actually was beneficial knowledge, then undoubtedly it must be from that which springs from the inherited guidance of Muhammad, may Allaah's praise and salutations be upon him. As there is nothing that can serve in its place as an alternative or substitute, from that which is considered similar to it or seen by some to be better than it.

Therefore, if his purpose and intent is to understand the goals and objectives of the Messenger of Allaah within everything that he commanded and that which he forbade, as well as in the rest of the Messenger's statements; and if his heart becomes satisfied with this understanding and the explanation of the rulings, this is the aim and objective of the Messenger's guidance. ...It is not possible to set straight or rectify the relationship between him and Allaah, the Most High as well as the relationship between him and the people, until he is capable of possessing this understanding. So struggle in every area of the various areas of knowledge to adhere to the foundation and fundamental knowledge which is transmitted directly from the Prophet, may Allaah's praise and salutations be upon him"[7]

---

[7]   Majmu'a al-Fatawaa: Vol. 19, page 119

Guide to the Symbols for Different Types of Texts or Citations Used with the Book

﴾ ﴿- (...) indicates a verse of the Qur'aan and the source surah of that verse.

{...}-(...) indicates a narration of the Messenger of Allaah, may Allaah's praise and salutations be upon him, or a narration from one of the first generations or one of the scholars.

The second set of brackets -(...) is where I have in a basic format referenced and indicated some but not all, of its sources as well as its similar supporting narrations, as many times these were not present in the original printed or audio sources. All stated rulings of authenticity are from Imaam al-Albaanee or Imaam Muqbil, may Allaah have mercy upon both of them, according to my limited ability. Similarly I have sometimes mentioned other relevant statements about the referred to narrations from these two distinguished scholars which I found in their books. Lastly, long source citations according to narrator have been separated from the text as numbered footnotes to facilitate reading. It should also be noted that the numbering systems of editions vary widely, and in newer printed or electronic editions the enumeration may differ.

[...] indicates an incorrect statement found among some of the common people or from the callers to falsehood whether from a book or tape.

In this text I have translated the original Arabic expression which is transliterated as, *'salla Allaahu aleihi wa sallam'* in reference to the Messenger of Allaah Muhammad Ibn 'Abdullah, according to the explanation found with the scholars of Ahlus-Sunnah wa al-Jama'ah. Its' meaning is explained in the compilation *'Salafee Selections from the Explanation of Aqeedah al-Waasiteeyah'*. Sheikh al-'Utheimeen, may Allaah the Most High have mercy upon him, stated on pages 114-115,

> *"As for the meaning of "salla Allaahu aleihi" the most accurate of what has been stated regarding this is what has been related from Abu Aleeyah, may Allaah have mercy upon him: 'It is Allaah's praise and commendation of him among the highest gatherings and assemblies in the heavens.'*
>
> *...And as for the meaning of "sallam" for him, within it is a statement of his being preserved from errors and shortcomings, and in the statement of "salat" upon him is an affirmation of his realization of the good characteristics and traits... So the single sentence with: "salat' and "sallam' contains an expression that informs but whose meaning is in fact one of asking or requesting by the speaker, as what is intended is supplication to Allaah.'*

Sheikh al-Fauzaan, may Allaah preserve, commented on page 116 of that same work:

> *"And the statement "salla Allaahu aleihi" linguistically carried the meaning of supplication; and the most authentic of what has been stated regarding the meaning of the "salat" from Allaah upon His Messenger is what Imaam al-Bukhaaree mentions in his Saheeh collection from Abu 'Aleeyah that he said: 'It is Allaah's praise and commendation of him among the highest gatherings and assemblies in the heavens.'... and the "sallam" means: salutations of honor or mention of his soundness and freedom from faults and failings'*

Therefore within this book its most common transliterated form, "*salla Allaahu aleihi wa sallam*" has been translated as: may Allaah's praise and salutations be upon him, and "*salla Allaahu aleihi wa alaa ahlehe wa sallam*" has been translated as: "may Allaah's praise and salutations be upon him and his household'.

Words of Thanks and Appreciation

I thank Allaah, Glorified and Exalted, for every blessing He has given me. I ask for good mention and prayers and blessings be upon the Prophet of mercy and the Messenger of guidance Muhammad and his family. I wish to thank our esteemed Sheikh Abu Nasr Muhammad Ibn 'Abdullah al-Imaam, may Allaah preserve him, as I occupied his valuable time on more than one occasion, seeking his assistance in the affairs of my deen....

I ask Allaah, Glorified and Exalted, to place me and every Muslim and Muslimah upon the path of beneficial knowledge and righteous actions, and to enable us to walk in the truly successful path as our pious predecessors did so that our knowledge a proof for us and not against us. May Allaah's praise and His salutations be upon our Prophet Muhammad and upon his family and Companions, and all those who follow his guidance until the Day of Judgment. And all praise is due to Allaah, Lord of the Worlds.

Written by Abu Sukhailah
Khalil Ibn-Abelahyi al-Amreekee

(*Abridged for Pocket Edition*)

(1)

THE DIFFERENCE BETWEEN KNOWLEDGE AND SPECULATIVE THOUGHT

Knowledge has tremendous benefits, the first of which is the rectification of one's worship. And "Islamic thinkers", as they have said, desire through their efforts to lead the people to a state of piety or to place them, as they say, upon a correct Islamic image or model; but this is not a guaranteed result. Rather this goal of theirs, in most cases, is not attained by them. However, true knowledge does indeed lead to the rectification of worship and towards piety.

This is because knowledge which is taken according to its principals, evidences, and fundamentals, upon the methodology of the first generations of Islaam, does guide to the rectification of one's worship, the establishing of firm and correct beliefs, and the correction of one's behavior and perspective in one's various dealings and interactions with the people, as well as in all newly occurring circumstances or situations.

As for speculative thought and opinion, then it changes constantly. Due to this, when the people do not have clear knowledge to direct and guide them, they frequently discuss and deliberate various matters at length such that new concepts begin to appear in their thoughts and speech. Ten or twenty different ideas or concepts are introduced at the same time, with each individual legitimizing and supporting his view, such that numerous differences and divisions then appear at a single gathering, with perhaps four people holding four separate and distinct views.

Likewise, one may hold a view and yet change it later, taking a differing view because speculative thought and opinion stands as the fundamental source or origin of that view. However, when we place knowledge as the fundamental reference, then the differing will be reduced and limited; it will be restrained such that the people will eventually reach the correct way of worship and the proper understanding.

From the greatest benefits or results of knowledge is that knowledge unifies while speculative thought causes separation. This fact was indicated in the statement of the former head religious authority of the country of Saudi Arabia, the exemplary scholar Sheikh Muhammad Ibn Ibraaheem, may Allaah have mercy upon him. In his time, he noticed the people drifting toward various cultural ideas and abandoning knowledge, and this was even before these different parties, groups, and organizations were known in this land- but close to the end of his life. So he made the following statement to some of the prominent individuals and some of the students of knowledge:

"I advise the people with knowledge, as knowledge unifies and speculative thought and unrestricted cultural ideas separate between you and cause disunity.' This is something true, which we have witnessed. Knowledge is that which unifies while unrestricted cultural ideas and concepts separate and lead to disunity. Consider that if you differ with someone on an issue and the fundamental source of reference for you both is knowledge. Everyone initially accepts his own understanding, saying, *"By Allaah, what is clear is that the ruling in this is such and such'* while another says, *"No. It is clear that the ruling in this is such and such.'* However after this they refer back to a scholar, eventually coming to unanimously agree on the correctness of his statement and judgment. Thus they are united after being previously divided in their views over this issue. And differing in relation to specific minor issues in understanding the religion is an easy matter. But how will the situation be if they were to differ in a serious issue- an issue related to the general welfare of the Muslim Ummah, or to the domain of calling to Allaah, or to the rectification of the matters through command and prohibition related to the struggle in the path of Allaah, or significant issues similar to these? In such a situation differing, if it occurs without referring back to the people of knowledge, leads to evil and separation.

The Muslim Ummah has taken a covenant that it would follow the Messenger of Allaah, may Allaah's praise and His salutations be upon him and his household, just as those who came before us followed their messenger or messengers, prayers and good mention be upon them all. As Allaah the High and Exalted says regarding the Christians: *And from those who call themselves Christians, We took their covenant, but they have abandoned a good part of the Message that was sent to them. So We planted amongst them enmity and hatred till the Day of Resurrection...*-(Surah al-Mai'dah:14) Meaning a covenant was taken from them that they would adhere to knowledge and abandon the opinions which they had conceived. Ibn Shihab az-Zuhree stated, *"The Jews and Christians did not go astray except through opinions."*

We see that there was taken from the Christians a covenant that they would adhere to knowledge; yet they partially adhered to that which they were given and in part they followed their own opinions. Thus, what happened is that they eventually separated and divided, and this separation is considered a punishment from the punishments of Allaah, as Allaah, High and Exalted, said, *And from those who call themselves Christians, We took their covenant, but they have abandoned...* meaning they left or turned away from it *they have abandoned a good part of the message that was sent to them* meaning from knowledge. Then they turned towards adherence to their opinions and their desires and so separated from each other. Allaah, High and Exalted, said, *So We planted amongst them enmity and hatred till the Day of Resurrection..*-(Surah al-Mai'dah:14)

This separation is not simply minor differing, but division which leads to hatred and enmity. Hatred emerges from it, and then envy emerges from it, and then more hatred which is outwardly or on the surface for Allaah's sake, but which is actually hatred resulting from this separation and division. The cause of their separation is the failure to adhere fully to knowledge from the very beginning, and their following of their own opinions, as what is truly knowledge brings unity, while unrestricted cultural ideas and concepts, and speculative thought causes separation. This is something readily apparent in the past history of the Muslim Ummah as well as in our modern history from what has occurred of the various types of division and disunity of concepts and ideologies among the various groups and societies, such that there is enmity between the various thinkers and writers. Thus it has progressed to the emergence of different schools of thought and distinct methodologies.

So we summarize by saying about the difference between knowledge and speculative thought, and what distinguishes between knowledge and speculative thought, is that knowledge is comprised of various types of evidence which are categorized and structured. As was mentioned by Qaraafee in his book *((al-Usooleeyah)08-10)*, there are thirteen types of evidence which are recognized, and in their detailed categorization, twenty types. This is opposed to speculative thought, whose evidences are neither categorized nor structured. Speculative thought may proceed in one case upon evidences of a specific thinker taking its origin in historical events, who then makes a determination or ruling derived from those past events upon other occurrences which are occurring in our time. But when can history itself be considered evidence? For example, a specific thinker states that the people from one specific land of the various lands, as is mentioned by the historians, the people of this land abandoned it due to the scarcity of sustenance or because of the harshness of the weather or a similar reason. They put this forth as a convincing demonstration or example, this being a principle from among their principles- the acceptability of the Muslims undertaking the same action.

So then they derive from these examples evidences for their idea or opinion. However, this idea or claim cannot be sound, nor is this opinion valid, because it was derived from an historical example as well as speculative thought which is not founded upon proper structured guidelines. So speculative thought is in fact unsystematic. Perhaps one person may make a statement and derive from that statement a result or conclusion. But the statement does not actually contain any valid evidenced explanation or support of that derived opinion. However, the statement will still be considered a correct and accepted explanation.

Another thinker comes and falsely concludes that the people who adhere to the hadeeth narrations are people who abandon commercial industry and turn away from entering into the various intellectual fields. They state that in the history of the Muslims these "people of hadeeth" did not produce anything worthwhile in the past or present, nor make any discoveries, nor contribute to literature- claiming these "accomplishments" were only produced by the intellectuals, meaning those who give precedence to intellect over revealed knowledge. They state that these intellectuals are the ones who promoted industry and furthered modern ideas and brought many advances to society, and it is their efforts which brought forth modern medicine and mathematics and so on, and none of this is known to have come from the people who adhere to the hadeeth narrations. In their view, this is proof that the way of thinking held by the "people of hadeeth" is incapable of leading the Muslim Ummah, and the methodology of the first three generations is incapable of guiding and directing the Muslim Ummah. Yes, they concede that in relation to limited "religious" rulings they are suited to bring forth their opinions.

However in relation to what would truly benefit the people- they hold that the people most suitable for that would be the people like the Mu'tazilah. Thus they believe that the Mu'tazilah are those truly suitable and capable of guiding the Muslim Ummah in the past and in the present age. They believe that the understanding of such "intellectuals", who give primary precedence to the role of the intellect is that which will actually enable the Muslim Ummah to advance. As for the people who adhere to revelation and hadeeth narrations or the scholars who explain the detailed rulings of the religion, then such people believe that their role is simply religious preaching.

Yet the historical assessment and analysis through which they derive this conclusion is reached through rejecting an essential fundamental from the foundations of correct belief in Islaam and through rejecting an evidence from the related evidences. This is that the group which the Messenger stated would be the continually "successful group" from among the Muslim Ummah is indeed those people who hold to the Sunnah of the Messenger of Allaah, and the Jama'ah -meaning those Muslims who remain united upon his guidance and those people of Sharee'ah knowledge. Such Muslims are indeed present today, and their people of knowledge assess every contemporary issue or problem, judging whether such and such matter in question is acceptable or not. Similarly, the true people of knowledge do not in any way prohibit manufacturing and production of goods, nor do they prohibit the various aspects of knowledge related to civilization.

If anyone did prohibit these, it would be due to a deficiency in his understanding or his distance from the correct understanding of the goals of the Sharee'ah. In fact it is only for the scholars to make such determinations for society, as they are also the doctors for our hearts, enabling the true advancement of the people toward the next life. Who else is available to establish the affairs within the

Muslim Ummah related to this worldly life, as well as to consider the various aspects of civilization, manufacturing, medical and engineering discoveries, and the principles of chemistry, astronomy, and physics and so on? They are the ones who will actually rule upon an endeavor which may possibly be undertaken by the Muslims: is this endeavor correct or incorrect? Furthermore, we do not merely mean from what has been mentioned that they are from one of the important foundations of society. Rather, the essential and prominent foundation of the religion is certainly the people of knowledge.

As such, the intellectual conclusions by this movement and its methodology of thinking are not based upon sound guidelines and principles, but are derived from merely viewing some aspects of history while at the same time rejecting a fundamental principal of the foundational beliefs as understood by the Sharee'ah. There has always been and will always be a group of Muslims present who are successful in understanding and practicing Islaam. Despite this deficiency there are some who have become satisfied with that false conclusion and circulate their beliefs concerning this issue.

Secondly from the important distinctions is that knowledge has set principles by which matters are assessed and weighed, and speculative thought lacks such principles by which questions and issues can be assessed. If an individual speaks regarding a knowledge-related issue, then we are able to judge whether his statement is acceptable or not acceptable. Are his statements strong or weak? But as for speculative thought, what then are its fundamental guidelines? What are its principles? If someone, meaning one of the general people, wishes to assess the statement of an intellectual thinker, with what standard can they assess it?? He is not able to refer it to accepted authorities to make a judgment or assessment.

However true knowledge in Islaam has such recognized authorities. In contrast, speculative thought is not established upon clear guidelines and principles nor does it have established authorities by which concepts can be evaluated, except by submitting itself to true knowledge. True knowledge acts as the judge and authority over speculative thought. Additionally, knowledge has as one of its essential characteristics that it is worthy of being commended and praised and that its people are worthy of commendation and praise. But as for speculative thought, it is simply various ideas and opinions, and the overall nature of opinion as held by the scholars is that it is condemned and censured. Indeed, this is a tremendous difference and fundamental distinction between these two matters.

[FROM 'KNOWLEDGE AND SPECULATIVE THOUGHT': PAGE 12]

(2)

THE IMPORTANT PLACE OF KNOWLEDGE
WITHIN AN INDIVIDUAL'S PRACTICE OF
THE RELIGION

Islaam is indeed the most important matter which an individual should commit himself to and adhere to. It is the most important matter he should struggle for and strive within himself towards realizing its reality. However, that is not possible except through knowledge. Indeed, beneficial knowledge is that which rectifies one's heart, and corrects one's actions and deeds. Indicating this, Allaah, the Most Perfect and the Most High, said,

This is my way; I invite to Allaah upon insight, I and whosoever follows me -(Surah Yusuf:108). The meaning of "upon insight' is upon and with knowledge.

As insight for the heart is knowledge which clarifies the reality of matters and shows what is correct within them. Allaah, the Most Perfect and the Most High, has said, *He who was dead without faith through his ignorance and disbelief and We gave him life by knowledge and faith and set for him a light (of Belief) whereby he can walk amongst men.* -(Surah al-Ana'am:122)

The people of knowledge state: "This 'light' is Islaam, which is both beneficial knowledge and righteous deeds. Due to this Allaah, the Most Perfect and the Most High, did not command His Prophet, may Allaah's praise and salutations be upon him, or his Ummah after him, to seek an increase in any matter except for an increase in knowledge. Allaah, the Most Perfect and the Most High, said in Surah Ta-ha: *Say my Lord increase me in knowledge.* Allaah has raised the people of knowledge over the rest of the believers due to what they have attained of knowledge. As He, the Most Perfect and the Most High, says, *Allaah raises those who believe from among you, and those who been given knowledge, by degrees* -(Surah al-Mujadalah:11)

So every believer has been raised by Allaah, the Most Perfect and the Most High, by his belief in Allaah, and, in addition to this, from within the ranks of the believers every true person of knowledge is further raised by his correct knowledge, such that the person of knowledge has been raised additional degrees over the others. This is from the blessings of Allaah the Most Perfect and the Most High upon the people of knowledge. If the student of knowledge pursues knowledge, and pursues this path of seeking knowledge, then Allaah makes easy for him the path to Jannah. As the Messenger of Allaah, may Allaah's praise and salutations be upon him, said in an authentic narration: *{Whoever goes forth upon the path of seeking knowledge, Allaah makes easy for him the path to Jannah.}* [1].

This is because the path to Jannah is realized by rectifying one's belief as well as by correcting one's deeds. And the rectification of one's beliefs is not possible except through knowledge. Likewise, the correction of one's actions is also only possible through knowledge. The statement, *{Whoever goes forth upon the path of seeking knowledge...}* means knowledge of the worship of Allaah alone, as well as knowledge of how to implement and practice the religion, and of the permissible and prohibited; consequently, *{... Allaah makes easy for him the path to Jannah.}* Since from the reasons of entering Paradise are the correctness of one's deeds, and the soundness of one's beliefs.

From the blessings of knowledge upon the scholar is that all of Allaah's creatures seek forgiveness for him, even the fish in the depths of the oceans. This is because he glorifies Allaah, affirms that there is none worthy of worship other than Him, extols Him, exalts and praises Him, and strives to follow and obey Him through Muhammad, may Allaah's praise and His

---

[1] Narrated in Saheeh Muslim: 2699/ Sunan at-Tirmidhee: 2945/ Sunan Ibn Maajah: 225/ & Musnad Ahmad: 7379- from the hadeeth of Abu Hurairah. Declared authentic by Sheikh al-Albaanee in Saheeh at-Targheeb wa al-Tarheeb: 69, 89, as well as in other of his books.

salutations be upon him; all this with certainty, knowledge, and understanding. By this that completion which is possible for creation may be attained. He becomes from amongst the highest of creation in merit, stature and closeness to Allaah, the Most Perfect and the Most High.

So by this we understand some aspects of the merit of the student of knowledge and the worth and position of the scholar, as all of Allaah's creatures seek forgiveness for him, even the fish in the depths of the oceans. Because all of these created things which Allaah, the High and Exalted, did not make responsible for their actions, comprehend the merit and blessing of the scholar who teaches the people good and the one who cultivates within the people the love of Allaah, the High and Exalted, and knowledge of His names and His attributes, and what is His right, High and Exalted is He, in terms of worshiping Him alone without partners and glorification of Him, and what is the right of His Prophet, may Allaah's praise and salutations be upon him, in relation to loving him and following him and knowledge of his Sunnah and adhering to it. When he becomes from those who spread the love of Allaah, High and Exalted, throughout the world, then by all this he surpasses the remainder of creation in merit. Because of this, every created thing seeks forgiveness for him, being pleased with the actions he puts forth, such that the angels lower their wings upon the student of knowledge due to their pleasure with his efforts, and due to the significance of his actions.

From this we see that, if one acts upon even some of these matters, then certainly he will receive a tremendous benefit from knowledge in relation to memorization, teaching, the attendance of circles of knowledge, as well as in understanding. Because no one desires these except the believer who has correct faith, and no desires to be far from these except every individual of separation and distance from the truth. Every person who struggles with himself in seeking knowledge, truly struggles in rectifying his heart and correcting his actions. Thus, the scholar or the student of knowledge if they fall into error, then their seeking forgiveness is not like the seeking of forgiveness of others. When they seek forgiveness, they are doing so upon knowledge and clarity, and the understanding of Allaah, the Most Perfect and the Most High, and what He requires from them, and understanding their own deficiencies, what they have indeed done and where they have fallen short in that.

So we see that the leader of the scholars of the Muslim Ummah after its Prophet, may Allaah's praise and salutations be upon him, Abu Bakr as-Siddeeq, may Allaah be pleased with him, was taught by our Prophet, may Allaah's praise and salutations be upon him, to supplicate in his prayers by saying, *{Allaah, certainly I have committed many injustices against my own soul, and there is no forgiveness of transgressions except through You, so forgive me as you are the One who Forgives, the Merciful.}* [2].

This supplication was for Abu Bakr as-Siddeeq, the most perfect follower in relation to his knowledge, deeds, behavior, characteristics, and his love and precedence in following the example of the Prophet, may Allaah's praise and His salutations be upon him! The Prophet taught him this supplication, which contains an extraordinary seeking of forgiveness and repentance from the standpoint of the significance in the acknowledgement of one's transgressions: *{My Lord, certainly I have committed many injustices against my own soul, and there is no forgiveness of transgressions except through you.}* [3].

[2]   Narrated in Saheeh al-Bukhaaree: 834, 6326, 7387, 7388/ Saheeh Muslim: 2705/ Sunan at-Tirmidhee: 3531/ Sunan an-Nasa'ee: 1303/ Sunan Ibn Maajah: 3835/ & Musnad Ahmad: 8, 29/ -from the hadeeth of Abu Bakr as-Saddeeq. Declared authentic by Sheikh al-Albaanee in Saheeh al-Jaame'a as-Sagheer: 7850, as well as in other of his books.

[3]   Narrated in Saheeh al-Bukhaaree: 811, 5977, 6975/Mustradraak al-Haakim: 2419, & other collections/-on the authority of Abu Bakr. And it is found in Saheeh Muslim: 1330/ Saheeh Ibn Hibaan: 2743/ & other collections -on the authority of Alee Ibn Abee Taalib. It was declared authentic by Sheikh al-Albaanee in al-Kalimah at-Tayyib, 172, Saheeh al-Jaame'a: 1821, 2069, Mukhtasir ash-Shama'el al-Muhammadeeyah: 198, and in other of his

Therefore, every student of knowledge and scholar, to the degree of his knowledge about Allaah, and his actions for the sake of Allaah, the High and Exalted, and his knowledge of the details of the Sharee'ah, and his knowledge of the rights of Allaah related to beliefs, is increased in his awareness of his sins and transgressions. So much so that he sees deeds of his as requiring the seeking of forgiveness, whereas another lacking that insight would not consider them matters which require the asking of forgiveness. For this reason, the level of the student of knowledge or the scholar is raised and increased according to the degree of knowledge they attain of the correct understanding of worshiping Allaah alone, and knowledge of the significance of their seeking forgiveness and repenting to Allaah, High and Exalted is He.

And in this age perhaps we may see that many people have mistaken ideas regarding knowledge from one perspective- or, actually, from several perspectives. They hold a mistaken idea regarding knowledge in that some think that knowledge does not possess benefits or rewards equal to what one sacrifices in its pursuit or in achieving it.

And there are those who hold the mistaken idea regarding knowledge that if you do strive for knowledge, at the end of your efforts you will still be just like any other person, not having obtained any significant results equal to your difficulties encountered in obtaining that knowledge. Then there are those who hold the mistaken idea regarding knowledge that the most important priority nowadays is calling and guiding the people, striving in this area, and similar efforts, believing that seeking knowledge does not have any significant effect or does not produce true results like these activities of calling and similar endeavors do.

works.

Additionally, there are those who hold the mistaken idea regarding knowledge that its attainment does not bring to the one who has acquired it any importance or significance in his status.

Rather, they believe that true importance is held by the people of worldly concerns, or those of the various other approaches and perspectives in this life.

All of these matters are actually from having mistaken ideas or concepts regarding the Sharee'ah itself, as knowledge is the Sharee'ah. So it is obligatory upon the student of knowledge to correct his understanding regarding Allaah, Glorified and High, to correct his thinking regarding acting according to knowledge, to correct his thinking regarding both knowledge and deeds collectively, and that he undertake all of this. How excellent is the saying of Ibn Qayyim, may Allaah have mercy upon him:

Ignorance is a mortal disease which is healed,

   with two complementary sources combined,

A text from Qur'aan or from the Sunnah

   and the doctor overseeing this cure is the guiding scholar.

Knowledge is divided into three, not having a fourth,

   the truth that which is contained in these two cures.

Knowledge of the description of His Loftiness and Ascendency and His actions,

   likewise of the names of the One who Judges after the Final accounting

As well as the commanding and forbidding as found in His religion,

   The reminding of the first separation death, as well as the second- that of the Day of the Hereafter and every matter from the Qur'aan and Sunnahs

which came to the one sent with the true criterion

By Allaah no eloquent one speaks from other than these two sources-

except for the one who is confused or simply delirious .

Additionally, one of the scholars said in ordered poetical verses, or rather composed poetry related to this, saying:

Do not have a bad opinion about knowledge, young man,

As bad suspicion about knowledge certainly leads to your ruin.

Indeed, this is the truth, as we have experienced and seen that every individual who has a mistaken or incorrect concept or idea regarding knowledge and so strays away from the path of traveling and seeking knowledge, and thus abandons it without continuing to seek knowledge- he does not achieve completeness. As knowledge is that which perfects the soul, and by it one's belief is perfected, and by it one's deeds are completed, and by it the ease and pleasure of the hearts is completed, and by it one's view and perspective of matters is perfected, and by it one completes the hope to do every matter according to the standards of the Sharee'ah. The people of knowledge mention that from the causes of the misguided people going astray within this Muslim Ummah is that they went astray because they were not established upon correct knowledge. This is because correct knowledge is a reason from among the reasons for the protection from trials and from the causes of misguidance and separation, as well as being a protection from other matters that are from the effects of abandoning knowledge.

Therefore I advise you and myself to preserve knowledge and preserve the memorization, examining, and carrying of knowledge, and that an individual should commit himself to studying it. Also, that he approaches what he does not know by taking knowledge of that matter from scholars about whom is known the reliability of their understanding of knowledge and their implementation of it. As through this, if Allaah, the Exalted wills, the rectification of the individual and of his actions will be realized. I ask Allaah, High and Exalted, to increase us and you in guidance and knowledge, and that He make us from truthful worshipers upon purity of intention for His pleasure alone, and that He forgives us our sins, as certainly He is free from all faults, the Bountiful, the Generous.

[FROM 'EXPLANATION OF THE MERITS OF ISLAAM': PAGES 2-3]

(3)

QUESTION: WHAT IS INTENDED BY THE STATEMENTS OF THE SCHOLARS OF THE FUNDAMENTALS OF THE RELIGION: "THE GENERAL PERSON SHOULD BLINDLY FOLLOW THE PEOPLE OF KNOWLEDGE." IS THE MEANING OF THIS THAT IT IS OBLIGATORY UPON THE GENERAL MUSLIM TO FOLLOW ONE SCHOLAR IN EVERY ONE OF HIS RULINGS, OR DOES IT MEAN SOMETHING ELSE? I HOPE FOR A CLARIFICATION OF THIS.

nswer: The meaning of 'taqleed' is blind acceptance and following of a statement by someone, when it is not considered one of the fundamental sources of the religion. It is acceptable by the agreement of the people of knowledge in its place with certain conditions. From these is firstly, the situation of the general person who has a question, but being a general person he does not understand the evidences nor the various derived rulings. Therefore it is obligatory for him to ask, as the Most Exalted and most High said, ❧*Ask the people of knowledge if you do not know* ❧-(Surah an-Nahl:43). So if he does not know the ruling of Allaah, Most Exalted and Most High, in a certain matter, then it is an obligation upon him to ask regarding it. And the general people are not all of the same type or description; rather, they are of different levels. One might be a student of knowledge, but is considered from the general people in regard to certain issues, as he does not know the rulings of these issues. So he must ask the people of knowledge regarding those and then act upon the rulings they guide him to in those issues.

As for the common person when asking, he should ask one of the people of knowledge whom he knows is reliable in his knowledge and religion. He should search in his land and ask others about who has the most knowledge and understanding, or he may find someone who he knows. Such that he says to himself, "*I am confident of this scholar's knowledge and practice of the religion.*" Then he should ask him whatever is necessary and act upon his advice. But it is not a fundamental concern nor required, meaning it is not an obligation upon the scholar, that he mention the evidence of his answer to the common person who asks him. This is the way of giving rulings proceeded upon by the Companions, may Allaah be pleased with them.

They issued rulings without always presenting the related evidence. Similarly, this way is reported from the practice of the leading scholars of Islaam, such as Imaam Maalik in his body of rulings, and Imaam Shaafa'ee in different issues, and Imaam Ahmad in various issues narrated from him. They gave rulings without mentioning the evidence; and this is something clear. Because it is an obligation to ask and inquire, but Allaah, The Most Exalted the Most High, did not make obligatory upon the people of knowledge to present the evidence, meaning to make clear the evidence to the one taking the ruling from him.

The second category of those who can blindly follow are the scholar and the student of knowledge; meaning that they accept the statement of one of the scholars without explicit evidence. If one needs to utilize such a statement because he does not have the time to investigate independently what the correct understanding in a specific issue is, and he is assured of this scholar's knowledge and his practice of the religion, then it is permissible to blindly follow him. So by agreement of the scholars, it is acceptable due to a situation where there is lack of time. Such as someone saying, *"Do I pray now or not pray? What should I do?"* So he asks one of the students of knowledge or a scholar who says to him: *"Pray now."* Then it is permissible upon him to blindly follow in this situation because of the absence of time to investigate, whether the one asked is a scholar or a student of knowledge. And the scholar can blindly follow the one who is more knowledgeable than him. This occurs frequently among the scholars of Islaam. Imaam Shaafa'ee would blindly follow Imaam Maalik in certain issues and then later change his stance, and Imaam Ahmad would blindly follow Imaam Shaafa'ee in a certain issue and than later change his position, and so on, as is well-known.

So if there is a situation where one's time is restricted but it is necessary for him to act, then he should not leave the matter to his own desires- that which he is inclined to do, or that he finds himself leaning towards without having the guiding words from a scholar. This includes an individual referring to what he has memorized from the knowledge based texts which explain how to practice the religion; such as what one might have memorized from *((Zaad al-Mustaqna')07-01)* and so forth.

Or one knows for a fact that a specific scholar has given a ruling in the issue that is being asked about, whether this is in an issue of purchasing, companionship, establishment of rights, or prayer. He is aware of the ruling but does not know from what evidence it is derived. Or perhaps one only remembers a scholar's statement in a knowledge-based text regarding the issue. Then one acts according to this recollection due to the condition of the limited time to verify and confirm the statement of the scholar because he has limited time available to research and what is correct in this issue, and related matters. So regarding the issue of blind following and the blind following of the common person, then the levels of independent investigation have several distinctions, and the levels among the common people vary greatly, so its discussion requires distinguishing between the people. This is presented to give a basic explanation, as discussing the details requires a considerable amount of time.

[FROM THE FRUITS OF KNOWLEDGE' QUESTION 3]

(4)

WO SIGNIFICANT OBSTACLES ON THE
PATH TO KNOWLEDGE

Also from these barriers is their saying, [Seeking knowledge diverts from calling to Allaah, and the people today need to be called to Allaah, but they do not have the same need for knowledge.]

This is a very dangerous claim which deadens one's efforts, and I know of many who have been afflicted in this way. These are those who say, [The knowledge of calling to Allaah is more important for us, along with associating with the youth, going with them, mixing and traveling with them to admonish them, or being engaged in some action or activity. As seeking knowledge doesn't bring results, or that the results from seeking knowledge come only after many years.] Indeed, this is a dangerous claim, and a significant barrier which impairs and weakens one's efforts. And it stems from a mistaken understanding regarding knowledge and deeds. The fundamental principle is that knowledge is one aspect or part and calling to Allaah is a separate part. However, knowledge does not come all at once, and calling to Allaah also is not done all at once.

So the student of knowledge, if he studies while also calling to Allaah according to the level of knowledge that Allaah has enabled him to acquire in this area, then he has established himself in knowledge as well as in bringing about good results through calling, to the level of understanding that he is given. But being diverted away from seeking knowledge by being busy with calling to Allaah simply causes one's calls to Allaah to be build upon ignorance. And this is what has afflicted many individuals.

In regard to this, the people have become three types:

Firstly, is one who is exclusively occupied in seeking knowledge, and he does not affect people beneficially at all.

Secondly is the one who turns to calling to Allaah while being ignorant or mostly ignorant of Allaah's religion.

So the first type of person is criticized and the second type is also criticized. This is because knowledge which does not bring good to the one who possesses it nor to others- is not considered beneficial, meaning to the people. As the student of knowledge, when he learns a little and then teaches it, preserves that knowledge with the Muslim Ummah. So if someone acquires knowledge, then his efforts in calling to Allaah should be to that level and degree of what that worshiper of Allaah has been given from knowledge. The endeavor of calling to Allaah is branches from knowledge which is its foundation. It is not possible for a worshipper to call to Allaah without knowledge.

As for the third type of person, he calls to that which he has learned, but he leaves off efforts of calling to those matters which he does not have knowledge of, as in doing that he would simply be like the one who blindly enters into that which he lacks knowledge of. Certainly, the Most High and Exalted says, ❖*Say "This is my way; I invite unto Allaah with 'al-baseerah', I and whosoever follows me*❖-(Surah Yusuf:108). The word '*al-baseerah*' means sure knowledge, ❖*I call to Allaah upon sure knowledge*❖. So it can be seen that knowledge is one necessary part, and similarly calling to Allaah is another additional part. Therefore, if you understand a matter according to its related evidences and it becomes clear to you, then you may call to that matter which you have learned according to what brings benefit to the people.

Some of the people believe that calling to Allaah encompasses nothing other than preaching, or presenting lectures, or travelling to villages, or giving speeches, and similar general activities in which one speaks with the people. But this is not correct. The prophets had the most complete and comprehensive call, and their statements were related to the highest matter of the right of Allaah, the Most High the Most Exalted, and singling Him out for worship alone. So if a student of knowledge teaches people then by this he is calling to Allaah. His teaching the people is in fact calling to Allaah, the Most High, the Most Exalted. He is calling himself as well as other than himself. However, the people have different situations and conditions, and what is facilitated for a person depends on the individual.

Imaam Maalik, may Allaah have mercy upon him, was asked about his exclusive dedication to knowledge, and his leaving of other areas of activity such as jihaad in the path of Allaah. He replied, "*Certainly from the people there are those whom Allaah has facilitated for them prayer, and there are those whom Allaah has facilitated for them the giving of charity, and there are those whom Allaah has facilitated for them the obligatory and non-obligatory pilgrimages, and there are those whom Allaah has facilitated for them striving in the path of Allaah, and there are those whom Allaah has facilitated for them knowledge. Indeed, Allaah has facilitated for me the matter of knowledge and I am pleased with that which Allaah has facilitated for me.*"

This narration remains to this day a reminder of the significant need of the people to remain upon beneficial knowledge.

Still, we should not permit the adopting of this dangerous deception concerning seeking knowledge, which is from the deceptions of Shaytaan: that one should prevent oneself from becoming occupied with knowledge because of the need to call to Allaah in more important. This was said by some of the people who came before us by fifteen years, and this is now twenty years later. When the years passed by, they become weak in their knowledge. They did not excel in seeking knowledge nor did they excel in calling people to Allaah. Knowledge is a weapon in your hand that you truly require and that you fight with, that you clarify and call to the truth with, to the degree of the knowledge Allaah the Most High, the Most Magnificent gives to you as His worshiper....

...Also from the obstacles upon the path of knowledge is the statement of the one who says, [Gaining knowledge requires a long period, dedication, and time, and I don't have the ability to dedicate myself to it or proceed as needed.] This is partially correct. It is true from the aspect that what is required is that knowledge remains with an individual. However, you do not know that which Allaah the Most High, the Most Magnificent will make possible or grant you the patience to accomplish. Moreover every breath of the scholar is in his favor and every step of the student of knowledge is written among his good deeds as he is engaged in a tremendous act of worship. How many people do not recognize within themselves a strong capacity to seek knowledge, then they seek knowledge and are patient in that until after some time they excel?! How many of those who had average or below average grades in school as now students of knowledge, benefitting the people?! While many of those who excelled in school are simply proceeding through life without benefiting anyone. Their previous achievements came to nothing.

The reason for this is as follows. One should know that seeking knowledge is a tremendously praiseworthy form of worship, if you understand that what is sought after is humbleness and the fruits that come from it, then according to the degree of their steadfastness in their continuing efforts- there will be results. Do not consider the time you spend in a gathering of knowledge or listening to a tape with the explanation of a book or a similar endeavor to be time wasted. Activities such as this will endow you with a love of knowledge and its people and will facilitate your acquiring knowledge step by step.

And it was mentioned to you the previous night, as is narrated by al-Khatteeb al-Baghdaadee in his book *((Jaam'ee Ahlaaq ar-Raawee wa Aadab as-Saame'a)04-11)* that one of the people of hadeeth said, "*There was a young man who was seeking knowledge of the hadeeth of the Messenger of Allaah and this became difficult for him. One day he passed by a place where there was a rock or stone, and he observed some water that streamed forth in small amounts, trickle after trickle, which had worn out a depression upon the stone where it flowed. He said to himself: "This is a lesson for you, oh so-and so. Your heart is not stronger than this stone, and knowledge is not weaker that this flowing water. So he returned and become one of the people of hadeeth and its narrators.*" This narration is transmitted authentically.

[FROM 'OBSTACLES IN SEEKING KNOWLEDGE']

(5)

QUESTION: I HAVE BEEN SEEKING KNOWLEDGE FOR SOME TIME; HOWEVER I DO NOT SEE ITS RESULTS UPON MYSELF OR UPON MY FAMILY EXCEPT TO A SMALL DEGREE. SO WHAT IS THE REASON FOR THIS, AND WHAT IS THE REMEDY FOR THIS SITUATION?

nswer: The fact that a worshipper who is a student of knowledge recognizes his shortcomings is itself from the fruits of knowledge. He recognizes that knowledge has not had a significant effect upon him, and also that it is necessary that he struggle within himself. This is indeed from the fruits of beneficial knowledge. Knowledge is something that must be facilitated for someone and not everyone will have facilitated for him the all various types of knowledge, and not everyone will have a specific type of knowledge made easy for him particularly. Likewise specific actions and deeds are not something which are facilitated for every individual. A man came to Imaam Maalik, may Allaah the Exalted have mercy upon him, and said to him,

"Oh our scholar and leader! We see from you every good matter, except that you do not make jihaad in the path of Allaah." *He replied, " Indeed, from the servants of Allaah there are those for whom He has facilitated the matter of prayer, and there are among the servants of Allaah those for whom He has facilitated the matter of fasting, and there are from the servants of Allaah those for whom He has facilitated the matter of pilgrimage to Mecca, and there are among the servants of Allaah those for whom He has facilitated the matter of jihaad, and there are from the servants of Allaah those for whom He has facilitated the matters of knowledge and teaching. I am from those for whom this last has been made easy and I am pleased by that which Allaah facilitated for me."*

The meaning of this is that it is difficult for an individual to establish efforts in every area or type of endeavor, which truly bear fruit and results. This is very difficult, and perhaps the one who was asked to realize this would not be able to fulfill and achieve it, meaning that it is very difficult to successfully seek knowledge in every branch of learning. A student of knowledge who for example, teaches others, always enjoins the good and forbids evil, always fulfills the rights of his parents and those of his children, as well as ensuring at every time to fulfill the general rights others have over him. The fact that these matters are so numerous makes it difficult for them to all be fulfilled by one person from among the people of knowledge. Yet, Allaah, the Most High the Most Exalted, has designated from His servants those who actually fulfill all of these varied matters. This is the position of the leading scholars, and they are rare in this Muslim Ummah. Their position is that of the revivers of the religion and so it is not proper for someone to place or consider himself at their level.

So if it is due this reason that you say, "I do not see the effects within me", then it is upon you to continue to struggle within yourself and not have disdain for yourself.

Do not say, [Knowledge is not benefiting me], or, [I cannot benefit through knowledge], such that you abandon seeking knowledge. No, as knowledge certainly is affected by the performance of the obligatory duties, the abandoning of forbidden acts, studying knowledge, and by beneficial speech.

An important factor may only have a small effect; however it will certainly have an effect upon your gaining knowledge. But if knowledge does not have any effect, meaning that the one who has acquired it performs forbidden acts, or falls into major sins, and from this we seek refuge with Allaah, or neglects the obligatory duties, or leaves giving the worshipers of Allaah their rights, or commits injustice against them in regard to their wealth, their possessions, or those prominent among them or something similar; then in this case, it is upon him to repent to Allaah, the Most High, the Most Exalted, and turn to him for assistance. As in this case knowledge brought forth evil results upon him. We ask Allaah, the Most High, the Most Exalted, for health and security.

[FROM 'FROM THE FRUITS OF KNOWLEDGE': QUESTION 2]

(6)

QUESTION: WHAT IS YOUR VIEW REGARDING THE ONE WHO EXPLAINS THE STATEMENT OF THE MESSENGER, MAY ALLAAH'S PRAISE AND SALUTATIONS BE UPON HIM, "WHOEVER ALLAAH INTENDS GOOD FOR HE GRANTS HIM UNDERSTANDING OF THE RELIGION", TO MEAN AN UNDERSTANDING OF WHICH ARE THE BEST OF ACTIONS TO SPEND YOUR TIME UPON, AND OF THOSE WHICH OF THEM POSSESSES THE GREATEST REWARD THAT WE SHOULD GIVE PRECEDENCE TO OVER OTHER RIGHTEOUS ACTIONS, AS THEY ARE OF GREATER BENEFIT TO US IN THAT SPECIFIC TIME?

nswer: This is correct; this is a accurate explanation of the hadeeth, and part of what this hadeeth indicates. Indeed, understanding and teaching the student of knowledge which good deeds have preference and priority is from beneficial knowledge. This means, for example, that such and such action is better and has more reward than this other deed. This requires knowledge and understanding. So if you inform him of that, there is no doubt that he will prefer and incline towards it, as it is better for him. Imaam Ahmad, may Allaah have mercy upon him, when al-Haafidh Abu Zur'ah UbaidAllaah Ibn 'Abdul-Kareem ar-Razee, who was well known, came to him, when he came to the city of Baghdaad, he would discuss and study hadeeth with him. He would discuss and debate with him regarding hadeeth from after salatul-'isha to salatul-fajr, because he only had come for a specific amount of days and he was one of the preservers of hadeeth.

They discussed and examined and memorized narrations, distinguishing and recognizing the weak ones from other than them, those with hidden defects, the fabricated ones and so forth. This benefited the Muslim Ummah tremendously, as during this time Abu Zur'ah was rarely in Baghdaad. Imaam Ahmad said, *"We substituted the praying at night with the sitting and discussion with Abu Zur'ah."* So he did not stand in prayer those specific nights of the visit, and did not pray these non obligatory prayers as was his custom. So he left his usual practice and only discussed hadeeth with Abu Zur'ah. There is no doubt that this action of his required knowledge and understanding.

This is from the understanding of the religion. As *{Whoever Allaah intends good for He grants him understanding in the religion.}* [1]. If a student of knowledge reaches a certain level of knowledge of the religion, he selects the most preferred action from the various preferred actions and the most commendable act from the praiseworthy acts from the various deeds of worship which are possible at a specific time. He chooses the preferred, and selects the most praiseworthy matter from the actions of merit available to him. So there is no doubt that this understanding of affairs is from what Allaah, the Most High, the Most Exalted, gives to some of his worshipers. This situation of priorities frequently reach him during the day and the night, for him this situation of choosing one matter over another is common. For example, the recitation of the Qur'aan before Salatul-fajr in the morning or asking Allaah for forgiveness. Which of these two is preferred?

Presently for many people it is something well known that they usually recite the Qur'aan before salatul-fajr in the morning, holding that this is better than seeking forgiveness. Yet many of the people of knowledge such as Sheikh al-Islaam Ibn Taymeeyah and leading scholars well known for efforts in calling to Allaah give precedence to seeking forgiveness at that time over other deeds, because this is from the guidance of the Prophet, upon him be the best mention in the heavens and the best of greetings. The Prophet, upon him be Allaah's praise and salutations, did not recite Qur'aan between the calling of the adhan of fajr and the call to begin the actual prayer,

---

[1]   Narrated in Saheeh al-Bukhaaree: 71, 3116, 7312/ Saheeh Muslim: 1037/ Sunan Ibn Maajah: 221/ al-Muwatta Maalik: 1300, 1667/ Musnad Imaam Ahmad: 16395: 16404, and other narrations/ Musannaf Ibn Abee Shaybah: 31792/ & Sunan ad-Daaramee: 224, 226/- on the authority of Mu'aweeyah. And it is found in Jaame'a al-Tirmidhee: 2645/ & Musnad Imaam Ahmad: 2786/ & Sunan ad-Daaramee: 270, 2706/- on the authority of Ibn 'Abbaas. And it is found in Sunan Ibn Maajah: 220/ Musannaf 'Abdul-Razzaaq: 30851/- on the authority of Abu Hurairah. It was declared authentic by Sheikh al-Albaanee in Saheeh al-Aadab al-Mufrad: 517, Silsilat al-Hadeeth as-Saheehah: 1194, 1195, 1196, Saheeh at-Targheeb at-Tarheeb: 67, as well as in other of his books. Sheikh Muqbil declared it authentic in al-Jaame'a al-Saheeh: 9, 3123, 4650.

Also the people who seek forgiveness fall under the general meaning of the statement of the Exalted, *those who pray and seek Allaah's forgiveness in the last hours of the night.*-(Surah Aal-'Imraan:17) and in the general meaning of the statement of the Most High, the Exalted, *They used to sleep but little by night. And in the hours before dawn, they were asking for forgiveness.*-(Surah adh-Dhaariyat:17-18) al-Hasan al-Basree, may Allaah the Exalted have mercy upon him, stated in explaining this verse, "*They would sleep only a little at night, and they would be frightened in the fear of their Lord. So when the morning came they sought His forgiveness having fear that their actions may not be accepted from them.*"

[FROM THE FRUITS OF KNOWLEDGE', QUESTION 6]

(7)

THE PERSONALITY OF THE STUDENT OF KNOWLEDGE AND ATTENDING LESSONS

The subject of our talk today is about the personality of the student of knowledge in regarding to attending lessons. As those who attend to listen to knowledge are different types. They differ from the aspect of their desire and eagerness for what they hear, and they differ in regard to their preparedness and readiness. Their levels of desiring and being eager for knowledge are not all comparable, nor are their degrees of readiness and preparedness all similar. Firstly, eagerness for knowledge is found to be at varying levels:

1. From them there is the one who listens to knowledge truly desiring to acquire or obtain it. This is the majority of them, and all praise is due to Allaah.
2. And from them there is the one who listens only wishing to make an estimation of that individual scholar, or to comprehend his level of knowledge, and the capacity of his ability to teach, or the degree of his aptitude in the areas of knowledge in general.
3. And among them is the one who attends a single time and then is absent for ten other instances.

These are some of their types, and within them there are those possessing different levels of desire, and we are assuming that these all are approaching knowledge truly desiring it. Therefore secondly, when the student of knowledge approaches a class or series of lessons desiring to benefit; it is necessary that he do so with a specific frame of mind and specific state of his heart, as well as possessing a certain intellectual mindset. As for the state of heart and the frame of mind it is that:

His intention in seeking this knowledge should be to remove himself from a state of ignorance. This is having sincerity in ones knowledge. Because the seeking of knowledge is worship, and it is an obligation to have a pure intention when doing so. Having sincerity in ones knowledge is intending that through learning it you will remove ignorance from oneself. Imaam Ahmad was asked about the intention one has in regard to knowledge, how should it be? He replied: "*It should be intended to remove ignorance from himself.*" As if you undertake seeking knowledge with the desire to become a teacher, a caller to the truth, an author, or something similar to that; then the correct and righteous intention in this and true sincerity in that is based upon two matters: Firstly, that the purpose is to remove ignorance from oneself, and secondly, that the purpose is to remove ignorance from others.

If one does not intend one of these two purposes, or both of them together, then he is not someone who possesses the correct intention. As if one of us aims to seek knowledge, then it is required that it be based upon the intention to remove ignorance from himself. And if you have such an intention then it naturally, must encompass various matters. Such as that Allaah, the Most High and exalted created him, and placed upon him commandments and prohibitions in the matter of most essential of all fundamentals and foundations- that being the right of the Most High, the Most Magnificent that He be worshiped alone without any partners or associates. Similarly, it encompasses understanding His commands and prohibitions in the permissible and impermissible matters; as well as comprehending the issue of recklessness of entering into prohibited matters in issues of belief.

Likewise, what is related to ignorant behavior and poor manners, and from the reasons of that is ignorance as well as other causes. So if he learns, he thus removes ignorance from himself, then he becomes someone with knowledge of what by Allaah the Most High, the Most Magnificent desires from him in life. Then after this, he must seek the assistance of Allaah the Most High, the Most Magnificent in conforming to the aims of His Sharee'ah, this is a personal matter related to this- that is essential.

A second personal matter that is also essential: is that when he seeks to acquire knowledge, he does so certain of the soundness of the knowledge possessed by his teacher. By this meaning that he is personally convinced that the basic state or condition of his teacher is that he teaches what is correct and sound. As if it comes to him in his thoughts that what the teacher teaches in in error, or that the information he conveys is mixed up and confused, or that he has this or that issue which would weaken his position or rank in knowledge; then the student will not benefit from this. Because as he sits and listens, his listening will be like that of a person who is reluctant to accept, having some objections to the one speaking. And so what occurs is that when such a teacher makes statement, a minute or half a minute after hearing it the listener will think and say to himself: *"This is correct and from the matters this scholar has strong understanding in."*. But then he thinks of such and such information which contradicts that statement just made by the teacher. Yet by the time he will have realized this, that minute has passed and the teacher has moved on to other matters. Likewise when the teacher ends that part of his explanation, the student hears another sentence, which is also seen as confused to him. Therefore more objections come forth, and this makes it impossible for the listener to properly take knowledge.

Rather, if there is something which seems to be incorrect within that which the student of knowledge hears, then he should have a paper or notebook in his hands in which he can write down the problem or issue; but then no longer think about it or consider it, just continue to listen to the knowledge of the lesson. He should just write in his notebook: *"investigate the issue of- such and such- later"*. Then when he is finished with that specific session, he should go that day or sometime afterwards and investigate this issue or ask regarding it. As from the matters which are well known is that it is not a required condition that a teacher be unquestionable and beyond mistakes, and it is not from the conditions that a teacher always be correct. As certainly he may take individual positions or views that differ from what is well known, or he may have recommendations or advice that he is mistaken in. However the issue or concern is that the teacher be witnessed or recognized to possess knowledge, connected to knowledge, having a sound understanding of what he speaks about. As if he understands what he speaks about, as well as the various statements of the people, and teaching beneficial knowledge; then he may lack comprehension in an specific issue, ruling, or similar matter. He may have mistakes in one instance, or regarding this concept, or something similar to this. And this is not something strange. As a teacher is human, and humans make mistakes. Accordingly, what is important is to take knowledge from the one that you are confident of his knowledge and that within yourself you have no about reservations about or objections to him. As this deprives many from a tremendous amount of knowledge, when they take knowledge with a mind set that is dubious or uncertain towards the teacher. Due to this the majority of questions that arise during a circle of knowledge, will not be answered.

Once we were present in a sitting with Sheikh 'Abdul-Razzaq al-'Afeefee, the well known guiding scholar, may Allaah the Exalted have mercy upon him. There was one there with him was asking him regarding some of the issues related to Hajj or the obligatory pilgrimage. Whenever someone came forth and asked the Sheikh for a ruling in a matter and the Sheikh replied; then one specific questioner would then come forward and say, "*Well, what if it was like this?*" He was attempting to learn knowledge by putting forwards additional issues other than the one the questioner originally asked regarding. Therefore the Sheikh, may Allaah have mercy upon him-said to him: "*Knowledge does not come in this manner, rather knowledge comes through studying it.*" And this is correct. Because the student as he spends time with the people of knowledge listening, if he exposes or opens his mind to it then perhaps with every issue which is raised -he asks something about it or every matter which he hears he immediately questions something in relation to it.

There have been many brothers and young men like this who passed along with us in the circles of knowledge. They put forth questions and problems that naturally come forth because of what they lack of knowledge. Due to this they put forward many such questions and problems, and if they had only been patient, that would have been better for them. This personality has an effect and influence upon ones intellect, and upon ones characteristics, and upon ones conception of areas of knowledge during lessons. Therefore it is required for us that when we take knowledge we take it with the mindset of someone who does not possess any knowledge.

We must listen, and listen, and listen, and if a difficulty in understanding arises, then we write it down and then investigate or ask regarding it later. Again, this naturally should be in relation to the teacher we feel an secure regarding his knowledge, so we are able to take knowledge from him having confidence in what he generally brings forth.

[FROM 'EXPLANATION OF KITAAB AT-TAWHEED': AUDIO TAPE 3]

(8)

QUESTION: DOES THE STUDENT OF KNOWLEDGE CONVEY ISLAMIC RULINGS TO THE PEOPLE ACCORDING TO WHAT HE HOLDS AS MOST CORRECT OR BY THE PREVAILING RULINGS IN THAT LAND?

nswer: This is a very significant and important issue because the student of knowledge engages in considering and reconciling positions within himself, such that it will become clear to him that some statements are sounder and more correct than others. Meaning the statement of Sheikh so-and-so is sounder in light of the evidence that he brings forth, and so he is content with that opinion, meaning with that particular ruling as opposed to others or with that statement rather than others. This is something which commonly occurs. If this happens, then the scholars have stated that the one who this occurs to should act according to this conclusion individually. This is due to the statement of Ibn al-'Abbaas to Sa'eed, *"How excellent is the one who stands upon what he has heard of knowledge transmitted to him."* If he personally acts upon his knowledge, then he has fulfilled his personal responsibility to Allaah, as he has realized and affirmed that knowledge.

As for the matter of issuing rulings to other people, then the general way of the Companions was to shift the issuing of rulings towards others from among them. It is not permissible for the student of knowledge to compete in giving rulings and be pleased with the people coming to seek rulings from him. Because issuing a ruling is as if you are saying that a signature of Allaah the Most Exalted, the Most High is upon that matter and it is unquestionably from the religion, meaning that you are conveying what is the ruling and judgement of Allaah the Most Exalted, the Most High. Therefore the worshiper of Allaah does not need to give a ruling and should direct the people to those who are qualified to give rulings who are present within that land; refer those seeking rulings to those individuals capable of issuing rulings. This is fulfilling your responsibility and is closer to goodness in relation to knowledge, actions, and the matter of issuing rulings.

If he is compelled to state a ruling due to the need presented to him, then he should not state a ruling that differs with what the people who issue rulings have already stated- meaning the people well-grounded in knowledge in his land where he lives. As the people proceeding and acting upon a single way is something which is desired in order to avoid the people's efforts to act upon the Sharee'ah being confused. The people would mock or try to subvert and pull down the Sharee'ah if it is seen to have different conflicting positions. This has, in fact, already occurred.

For example, some of the people made independent judgements or rulings, perhaps within the different sunnahs of the ritual prayer or something similar. But the general people do not understand that in some matters there are acceptable differences based upon evidence; they don't understand this. So then they begin to doubt the general validity of the action itself, or the scholar who issued the general ruling, or this student of knowledge and what action he is doing, or they have doubts about the religion in general. He says in this area there is wide latitude so do whatever you want, this is not something crucial. There is no doubt that this result has many forms of corruption related to it. For this reason, the scholars of this land and the leading scholars of the call to adhere to the Qur'aan and Sunnah first and foremost, may Allaah the Most High have mercy upon them, prohibited an individual who has not been charged with giving rulings from issuing rulings generally for the people. But the one who, after consideration of the evidences, concludes for himself what he believes is the strongest and soundest position, can act upon this individually. But those who give ruling to others generally should only be those who are charged with putting forth rulings.

[FROM 'THE FRUITS OF KNOWLEDGE': QUESTION 4]

(9)

QUESTION: WE REQUIRE A GOOD METHOD
FOR READING BOOKS. IS IT ENOUGH
TO READ THEM A SINGLE TIME OR IS IT
NECESSARY TO REREAD BOOKS? IF THIS IS
INDEED NECESSARY, HOW IS THIS POSSIBLE
CONSIDERING THE LARGE NUMBER OF BOOKS?

nswer: The method of reading of books differs as some books are books of fundamental and essential knowledge, these perhaps should be read two or three times. While with other books this is not done, as they are simply reffered to once when needed. An example would be *((Tayseer al-Azeez al-Hameed Fath al-Majeed)06-20)*, this book is one that deserves be read a number of times, as it is a book of fundamental principles. And *((Sharh al-Waasiteeyyah)06-21)* by Sheikh Ibn Rasheed, may Allaah have mercy upon him, or for example *((Sharh al-Tahaweeyah)06-09)*. These works are important, so if you many times then that is fine. This is also the case with the explanation *(Sharh al-Badhur)03-07)*, or the explanations of *((az-Zaad)07-01)* or *((al-Hawasha)07-27)* there is no harm in rereading them, rather it is in fact better to read them several times.

However works such as *(Fath al-Baaree)03-01)* should be gone through in a similar way to *(al-Mughnee al-Kafee)07-07)* meaning until you reach its end, completing it fully once. But neither of this books are from those which needs to be read repeatedly. Therefore some of the books it may be possible for you to reread them, and some are turned to only when needed or used for reference, this is what is intended.

[FROM 'EXPLANATION OF AL-AQEEDATUT-TAHAAWEYAH': LESSON 42]

(10)

PRESERVING EXCERPTS

OF KNOWLEDGE

All praise is due to Allaah, may Allaah's praise and salutations upon the Messenger of Allaah, and upon his family, his Companions, and all those who followed his guidance. As for what follows:

Indeed I ask Allaah, the Most Exalted, the Most Magnificent, for myself and for you - beneficial knowledge and righteous deeds, and that He bless us to work in those matters with which He loves and is pleased. And that He make our knowledge a proof for us and not against us on that final Day of Reckoning.

Certainly from among the important matters related to the student of knowledge proceeding in his studies is his giving attention to the preservation of knowledge through writing down notes and recording passages. What I intend by preserving knowledge through writing notes are those notes which one searches for in books, or which one hears from the scholars, the people of knowledge, or the students of knowledge. This latter is due to the fact that studying and taking knowledge from individuals has additional benefits which the majority of people will not find when simply studying books. For this reason it is necessary that you record them, and this means writing them down in a specific notebook. It is something rare that you would find one of the people of knowledge who did not have from his previous years of seeking knowledge a specific notebook for this, or collected papers where he had written down what he collected of important things which he read or heard from the scholars. As if you read you will always encounter many things which are not remarkable or which you do not have a significant need for which you simply leave it as it is. Yet sometimes when reading you will encounter points and benefits which are important, and similarly in what you hear from the scholars, or from your teachers.

There are matters which are important and there are matters which are general descriptions or explanations, and these general descriptions can be understood by referring back to available reference works or something similar. But as for that which is related to definitions, classifications, or conceptualizations, the mentioning of scholastic differences, what are the strongest position in various issues, the mentioning of the evidence of issues, or the direction of derivation of matters- then for these types of benefits it is required that you record them. Therefore, it becomes a requirement of study that you designate a specific notebook to write down such benefits which are heard from others or read. That which I mean should be written down in this notebook or note pad is that which you specifically use for writing down definitions and knowledge based precepts and principles, as knowledge is defined within definitions and knowledge based principles, so that one should be concerned with mentioning their restrictions and limits. If you hear mentioned a restriction in the application of a specific matter, then certainly that restriction has an essential importance like the importance of fundamental validity and basis of that issue. Without comprehending that crucial restriction your understanding of the foundation and basis of the issue will not be sound. It will likely be flawed and so you would apply it in other than its proper place. Similar is the matter of categorization, as you will find that in many of the books of the people of knowledge they state that this matter is divided into three categories, or this concept has three types of occurrences, or five, or it is mentioned that it has two categories which are each divided further into two more categories each. Ibn Qayyim may Allaah, the Most High have mercy upon him, said: *"Knowledge is comprehended through understanding it divisions and categories."*

Then your intellect can understand it well. Indeed, from verification is returning back to the correcting understanding of the basic definition, and reliably applying the boundaries upon properly understanding the divisions and categories in that area of knowledge. If you see in the statements of the people of knowledge that this matter is divided into this section and that section, then it is important that you write this down, or study it and preserve your understanding of this categorization.

Also among the important matters related to your proceeding in seeking knowledge regarding what you have recorded and written down is that you regularly reevaluate and review what you have written down in your notebook or notebooks. You will find, for example, that after a year of seeking knowledge some of what you had written down in that year will seem strange to you after the time has gone by. Why? Because at the time that you wrote them down, many of those issues were new and unfamiliar to you, so therefore you wrote them down in order to remember them. Yet after having remembered them, and then studying the subject, and previously repeatedly going over what you had written, the subject becomes as clear and understandable as your own name is to you. Subsequently, your understanding of matter increases, and whenever your understanding of that which you previously memorized increases, then it all becomes more clear to you, and there is no hardship in comprehending it. This is because it has become firmly imprinted and memorized in your mind, with all of its details and points.

For these reasons it is important that you train yourself to record and write down important notes about that which you hear or read in those aspects of knowledge which we have mentioned, either definition, or divisions and categorizations, or evidences, or the direction of how such evidences where derived.

And this encompasses all the various areas and branches of knowledge, whether that be area of industrial and manufacturing sciences, or the fundamental religious sciences, which are what was originally intended. How excellent it would be if you started to undertake this way of preserving your knowledge this very day. So go and make for yourself a notebook for recording benefits, and then strive to memorize them. After some time you will find that these issues have become easy and understandable to you, and you can then proceed to other aspects or areas of study and so gather a good portion of knowledge after a time. I ask Allaah the Most Exalted, the Most Magnificent, to make us and to make you from among those whom he has made easy for use the gaining of knowledge and the building upon that knowledge with deeds. May the praise and salutations be upon our prophet Muhammad.

[FROM 'EXPLANATION OF KITAAB AT-TAWHEED': AUDIO CASSETTE 2]

THE NAKHLAH EDUCATIONAL SERIES:

MISSION

The Purpose of the 'Nakhlah Educational Series' is to contribute to the present knowledge based efforts which enable Muslim individuals, families, and communities to understand and learn Islaam and then to develop within and truly live Islaam. Our commitment and goal is to contribute beneficial publications and works that:

Firstly, reflect the priority, message and methodology of all the prophets and messengers sent to humanity, meaning that single revealed message which embodies the very purpose of life, and of human creation. As Allaah the Most High has said,

❧ *We sent a Messenger to every nation ordering them that they should worship Allaah alone, obey Him and make their worship purely for Him, and that they should avoid everything worshipped besides Allaah. So from them there were those whom Allaah guided to His religion, and there were those who were unbelievers for whom misguidance was ordained. So travel through the land and see the destruction that befell those who denied the Messengers and disbelieved.*❧ –(Surah an-Nahl: 36)

Secondly, building upon the above foundation, our commitment is to contributing publications and works which reflect the inherited message and methodology of the acknowledged scholars of the many various branches of Sharee'ah knowledge who stood upon the straight path of preserved guidance in every century and time since the time of our Messenger, may Allaah's praise and salutations be upon him. These people of knowledge, who are the inheritors of the Final Messenger, have always adhered closely to the two revealed sources of guidance: the Book of Allaah and the Sunnah of the Messenger of Allaah- may Allaah's praise and salutations be upon him, upon the united consensus, standing with the body of guided Muslims in every century - preserving and transmitting the true religion generation after generation. Indeed the Messenger of Allaah, may Allaah's praise and salutations be upon him, informed us that, *{ A group of people amongst my Ummah will remain obedient to Allaah's orders. They will not be harmed by those who leave them nor by those who oppose them, until Allaah's command for the Last Day comes upon them while they remain on the right path. }* (Authentically narrated in Saheeh al-Bukhaaree).

The guiding scholar Sheikh Zayd al-Madkhalee, may Allaah protect him, stated in his writing, 'The Well Established Principles of the Way of the First Generations of Muslims: It's Enduring & Excellent Distinct Characteristics' that,

"From among these principles and characteristics is that the methodology of tasfeeyah -or clarification, and tarbeeyah -or education and cultivation- is clearly affirmed and established as a true way coming from the first three generations of Islaam, and is something well known to the people of true merit from among them, as is concluded by considering all the related evidence.

What is intended by tasfeeyah, when referring to it generally, is clarifying that which is the truth from that which is falsehood, what is goodness from that which is harmful and corrupt, and when referring to its specific meanings it is distinguishing the noble Sunnah of the Prophet and the people of the Sunnah from those innovated matters brought into the religion and the people who are supporters of such innovations.

As for what is intended by tarbeeyah, it is calling all of the creation to take on the manners and embrace the excellent character invited to by that guidance revealed to them by their Lord through His worshiper and Messenger Muhammad, may Allaah's praise and salutations be upon him; so that they might have good character, manners, and behavior. As without this they cannot have a good life, nor can they put right their present condition or their final destination. And we seek refuge in Allaah from the evil of not being able to achieve that rectification."

Thus the methodology of the people of standing upon the Prophet's Sunnah, and proceeding upon the 'way of the believers' in every century is reflected in a focus and concern with these two essential matters: tasfeeyah or clarification of what is original, revealed message from the Lord of all the worlds, and tarbeeyah or education and raising of ourselves, our families, and our communities, and our lands upon what has been distinguished to be that true message and path.

The Roles of the Scholars & General Muslims In Raising the New Generation

The priority and focus of the 'Nakhlah Educational Series' is reflected within in the following statements of Sheikh al-Albaanee, may Allaah have mercy upon him:

"As for the other obligation, then I intend by this the education of the young generation upon Islaam purified from all of those impurities we have mentioned, giving them a correct Islamic education from their very earliest years, without any influence of a foreign, disbelieving education."

(Silsilat al-Hadeeth ad-Da'eefah, Introduction page 2.)

"...And since the Messenger of Allaah, may Allaah's praise and salutations be upon him, has indicated that the only cure to remove this state of humiliation that we find ourselves entrenched within, is truly returning back to the religion. Then it is clearly obligatory upon us - through the people of knowledge- to correctly and properly understand the religion in a way that conforms to the sources of the Book of Allaah and the Sunnah, and that we educate and raise a new virtuous, righteous generation upon this."

(Clarification and Cultivation and the Need of the Muslims for Them)

It is essential in discussing our perspective upon this obligation of raising the new generation of Muslims, that we highlight and bring attention to a required pillar of these efforts as indicated by Sheikh al-Albaanee, may Allaah have mercy upon him, and others- in the golden words, "*through the people of knowledge*". Since something we commonly experience today is that many people have various incorrect understandings of the role that the scholars should have in the life of a Muslim, failing to understand the way in which they fulfill their position as the inheritors of the Messenger of Allaah, may Allaah's praise and salutations be upon him, and stand as those who preserve and enable us to practice the guidance of Islaam. Similarly the guiding scholar Sheikh 'Abdul-'Azeez Ibn Baaz, may Allaah have mercy upon him, also emphasized this same overall responsibility:

"...It is also upon a Muslim that he struggles diligently in that which will place his worldly affairs in a good state, just as he must also strive in the correcting of his religious affairs and the affairs of his own family. As the people of his household have a significant right over him that he strive diligently in rectifying their affair and guiding them towards goodness, due to the statement of Allaah, the Most Exalted, ◈ Oh you who believe! Save yourselves and your families Hellfire whose fuel is men and stones ◈ -(Surah at-Tahreem: 6)

So it is upon you to strive to correct the affairs of the members of your family. This includes your wife, your children- both male and female- and such as your own brothers. This concerns all of the people in your family, meaning you should strive to teach them the religion, guiding and directing them, and warning them from those matters Allaah has prohibited for us. Because you are the one who is responsible for them as shown in the statement of the Prophet, may Allaah's praise and salutations be upon him, { Every one of you is a guardian, and responsible for what is in his custody. The ruler is a guardian of his subjects and responsible for them; a husband is a guardian of his family and is responsible for it; a lady is a guardian of her husband's house and is responsible for it, and a servant is a guardian of his master's property and is responsible for it....} Then the Messenger of Allaah, may Allaah's praise and salutations be upon him, continued to say, *{...so all of you are guardians and are responsible for those under your authority.}* (Authentically narrated in Saheeh al-Bukhaaree & Muslim)

It is upon us to strive diligently in correcting the affairs of the members of our families, from the aspect of purifying their sincerity of intention for Allaah's sake alone in all of their deeds, and ensuring that they truthfully believe in and follow the Messenger of Allaah, may Allaah's praise and salutations be upon him, their fulfilling the prayer and the other obligations which Allaah the Most Exalted has commanded for us, as well as from the direction of distancing them from everything which Allaah has prohibited.

It is upon every single man and women to give advice to their families about the fulfillment of what is obligatory upon them. Certainly, it is upon the woman as well as upon the man to perform this. In this way our homes become corrected and rectified in regard to the most important and essential matters. Allaah said to His Prophet, may Allaah's praise and salutations be upon him, ﴾ **And enjoin the ritual prayers on your family...** ﴿ (Surah Taha: 132) Similarly, Allaah the Most Exalted said to His prophet Ismaa'aeel, ﴾ **And mention in the Book, Ismaa'aeel. Verily, he was true to what he promised, and he was a Messenger, and a Prophet. And he used to enjoin on his family and his people the ritual prayers and the obligatory charity, and his Lord was pleased with him.** ﴿ -(Surah Maryam: 54-55)

As such, it is only proper that we model ourselves after the prophets and the best of people, and be concerned with the state of the members of our households. Do not be neglectful of them, oh worshipper of Allaah! Regardless of whether it is concerning your wife, your mother, father, grandfather, grandmother, your brothers, or your children; it is upon you to strive diligently in correcting their state and condition..."

(Collection of Various Rulings and Statements- Sheikh 'Abdul-'Azeez Ibn 'Abdullah Ibn Baaz, Vol. 6, page 47)

We hope to contribute works which enable every striving Muslim who acknowledges the proper position of the scholars, to fulfill the recognized duty and obligation which lays upon each one of us to bring the light of Islaam into our own lives as individuals as well as into our homes and among our families. Towards this goal we are committed to developing educational publications and comprehensive educational curriculums -through cooperation with and based upon the works of the scholars of Islaam and the students of knowledge. Works which, with the assistance of Allaah, the Most High, we can utilize to educate and instruct ourselves, our families and our communities upon Islaam in both principle and practice. The publications and works of the Nakhlah Educational Series are divided into the following categories:

Basic: Ages 4- 6

Elementary: Ages 6-11

Secondary: Ages 11-14

High School: Ages 14- Young Adult

General: Young Adult –Adult

Supplementary: All Ages

Publications and works within these stated levels will, with the permission of Allaah, encompass different beneficial areas and subjects, and will be offered in every permissible form of media and medium. As certainly, as the guiding scholar Sheikh Saaleh Fauzaan al-Fauzaan, may Allaah preserve him, has stated,

"Beneficial knowledge is itself divided into two categories. Firstly is that knowledge which is tremendous in its benefit, as it benefits in this world and continues to benefit in the Hereafter. This is religious Sharee'ah knowledge. And secondly, that which is limited and restricted to matters related to the life of this world, such as learning the processes of manufacturing various goods. This is a category of knowledge related specifically to worldly affairs.

...As for the learning of worldly knowledge, such as knowledge of manufacturing, then it is legislated upon us collectively to learn whatever the Muslims have a need for. Yet If they do not have a need for this knowledge, then learning it is a neutral matter upon the condition that it does not compete with or displace any areas of Sharee'ah knowledge..."

("Explanations of the Mistakes of Some Writers'", Pages 10-12)

We ask Allaah, the most High to bless us with success in contributing to the many efforts of our Muslim brothers and sisters committed to raising themselves as individuals and the next generation of our children upon that Islaam which Allaah has perfected and chosen for us, and which He has enabled the guided Muslims to proceed upon in each and every century. We ask him to forgive us, and forgive the Muslim men and the Muslim women, and to guide all the believers to everything He loves and is pleased with. The success is from Allaah, The Most High The Most Exalted, alone and all praise is due to Him.

Abu Sukhailah Khalil Ibn-Abelahyi
Taalib al-Ilm Educational Resources

BOOK PUBLICATION PREVIEW:

Statements of the Guiding Scholars of Our Age Regarding Books & their Advice to the Beginner Seeker of Knowledge

with Selections from the Following Scholars:
Sheikh 'Abdul-'Azeez ibn 'Abdullah ibn Baaz -Sheikh Muhammad ibn Saaleh al-'Utheimein - Sheikh Muhammad Naasiruddeen al-Albaanee - Sheikh Muqbil ibn Haadee al-Waada'ee - Sheikh 'Abdur-Rahman ibn Naaser as-Sa'adee - Sheikh Muhammad 'Amaan al-Jaamee - Sheikh Muhammad al-Ameen as-Shanqeetee - Sheikh Ahmad ibn Yahya an-Najmee & Sheikh Saaleh al-Fauzaan ibn 'Abdullah al-Fauzaan - Sheikh Saaleh ibn 'Abdul-'Azeez Aal-Sheikh - Sheikh Muhammad ibn 'Abdul-Wahhab al-Wasaabee -Permanent Committee to Scholastic Research & Issuing Of Islamic Rulings

With an introduction by: Sheikh Muhammad Ibn 'Abdullah al-Imaam
Collected and Translated by Abu Sukhailah Khalil Ibn-Abelahyi al-Amreekee

[Available: **Now** ¦ pages: 370+ ¦ price: (S) **$25** (H) **$32** ¦ eBook **$9.99**]

SCAN WITH SMARTPHONE

FOR MORE INFORMATION

SCAN WITH SMARTPHONE

FOR MORE INFORMATION

BOOK PUBLICATION PREVIEW:

Al-Waajibaat:
The Obligatory Matters

What it is Decreed that Every Male and Female Muslim Must Have Knowledge Of -from the statements of Sheikh al-Islaam Muhammad ibn 'Abdul-Wahaab

(A Step By Step Course on The Fundamental Beliefs of Islaam- with Lesson Questions, Quizzes, & Exams)

Collected and Arranged by
Umm Mujaahid Khadijah Bint Lacina
al-Amreekiyyah

[Available: **Now - Self Study/ Teachers Edition**
price: (Soft cover) **$20** (Hard cover) **$27**
Directed Study Edition price: **$17.50** -
Exercise Workbook price: **$10** ¦ eBook **$9.99**]

SCAN WITH SMARTPHONE

FOR MORE INFORMATION

SCAN WITH SMARTPHONE

FOR MORE INFORMATION

BOOK PUBLICATION PREVIEW:

Fasting from Alif to Yaa:

A Day by Day Guide to Making the Most of Ramadhaan

-Contains additional points of benefit to teach one
how to live Islaam as a way of life
-Plus, stories of the Prophets and Messengers
including activities for the whole family to enjoy
and benefit from for each day of Ramadhaan. Some
of the Prophets and Messengers covered include
Aadam, Ibraaheem, Lut, Yusuf, Sulaymaan, Shu'ayb,
Moosa, Zakariyyah, Muhammad, and more!
-Recipes for foods enjoyed by Muslims around the
world

By Umm Mujaahid Khadijah Bint Lacina al-
Amreekiyyah as-Salafiyyah With Abu Hamzah
Hudhaifah Ibn Khalil and Umm Usaamah Sukhailah
Bint Khalil

[Available: **1433** -pages: 250+ ¦ price: (S) **$20** (H) **$27** ¦
eBook **$9.99**

SCAN WITH SMARTPHONE

PRINT

FOR MORE INFORMATION

SCAN WITH SMARTPHONE

EBOOK

FOR MORE INFORMATION